Young Pocahontas

Indian Princess

A Troll First-Start Biography

by Anne Benjamin
illustrated by Christine Powers

Troll Associates

Pocahontas

Library of Congress Cataloging-in-Publication Data

Benjamin, Anne.
    Young Pocahontas: Indian princess / by Anne Benjamin;
illustrated by Christine Powers.
        p.   cm.—(First-start biographies)
    Summary: A simple biography of the seventeenth-century Indian
princess who befriended Captain John Smith and the English settlers
of Jamestown.
    ISBN 0-8167-2534-9 (lib. bdg.)   ISBN 0-8167-2535-7 (pbk.)
    1. Pocahontas, d. 1617—Juvenile literature.   2. Powhatan Indians—
Biography—Juvenile literature.   3. Jamestown (Va.)—History—
Juvenile literature. [1. Pocahontas, d. 1617.   2. Powhatan
Indians—Biography.   3. Indians of North America—Biography.
4. Jamestown (Va.)—History.]   I. Powers, Christine, ill.
II. Title.   III. Series.
E99.P85P5715   1992
975.5'01'092—dc20
[B]   91-32654

Pocahontas was a young girl who helped the first English settlers in America.

Pocahontas was born in Virginia about 1595. Her father, Powhatan, was a powerful Indian chief.

Powhatan could be very cruel.
But he loved his pretty little daughter.
He named her Pocahontas, which
meant "playful one."

Growing up was fun for Pocahontas.
She ran and played through the woods
and meadows.

Each morning Pocahontas and the other villagers ran down to the river to say hello to the sun.

And each morning Pocahontas jumped
into the river for a bath. She even did
this in the winter!

When Pocahontas was about 12 years old, life in the woods suddenly changed. The first English settlers came to Virginia. They built a small colony, which they named Jamestown.

The Indians had never seen people
like this before. They were afraid of
the settlers.

One day Powhatan's men captured
John Smith. He was one of
Jamestown's leaders. They brought
him to the Indian village.

Powhatan decided to kill Captain
Smith. The Indians held Smith's head
down on a stone. Then they gathered
around him, holding heavy clubs. In
just a few moments, Captain Smith
would die.

Suddenly, Pocahontas ran through the crowd and laid her head upon Smith's. She begged her father to spare Smith's life.

Because there was an old Indian
custom that said a woman could save a
prisoner's life, Powhatan had to agree.

Captain Smith stayed with the Indians
for a while. He and Pocahontas became
good friends. Smith gave her presents
and told her stories about England.

The English settlers and the Indians
lived side by side for 2 years. But
things were not always peaceful.

Pocahontas visited Jamestown often.
She brought the settlers food when
they had none. Without her help,
the settlers might have died.

In 1609, Captain Smith went back to England. Pocahontas stopped visiting the colony.

When Pocahontas was 18, more trouble broke out between the settlers and the Indians. The settlers kidnapped Pocahontas and brought her to Jamestown.

In Jamestown, Pocahontas met John
Rolfe. Soon they fell in love. In 1614,
John and Pocahontas got married.

25

Pocahontas had a son named Thomas.
She was very happy with her new
family.

In England, many people had heard
about Pocahontas. They wanted to
meet the Indian princess. So the
Rolfe family decided to visit London.

Pocahontas met many people in London, even the king and queen. And she was amazed by all of London's markets and shops.

But the best part of her trip was
seeing her old friend Captain Smith
again. They talked for hours.

Finally the Rolfes decided to go back to Virginia. But before they could leave, Pocahontas got very sick. She died when she was only 21.

Pocahontas' life was short, but
important. Thanks to her, the
Jamestown colony was a success.

jB
POCAHONT
A

Benjamin, Anne

Young Pocahontas

467139

$10.79

93   98

DEC - 7 1992

SOUTH HUNTINGTON
PUBLIC LIBRARY
2 MELVILLE ROAD
HUNTINGTON STATION, N.Y. 11746

BAKER & TAYLOR BOOKS